40 DAYS WITH
THE GOSPEL OF MATTHEW,
VOL. 1

A 40-DAY BIBLICAL
DEVOTIONAL JOURNAL:
STUDY • REFLECT • DISCERN • PRAY

40 Days With…The Gospel of Matthew, Vol. 1
A 40-Day Biblical Devotional Journal: Study Reflect Discern Pray

ISBN: 978-1-945056-26-0

Printed in the United States

Book Design: Velin@Perseus-Design.com

Cover photo credits: magagraphics / Depositphotos.com

PREFACE

As a pastor, I am a big fan of daily devotions. Dedicated time reflecting on Scripture helps me grow in my faith and often helps me keep my daily life in a proper perspective. I have used many different devotionals through the years. This series of devotionals was developed in an attempt to address a few shortcomings I have encountered in devotionals currently available.

- Many devotionals are 365 days. Sometimes, I simply cannot or do not want to make a 365 day commitment to one devotional. Sometimes I want or need to focus my devotion time in another direction for a season – for example, maybe I want to use an Advent devotional. Sometimes, I fall behind a few days and then it becomes a chore to catch up, or I skip the missed days and might lose some of the intended devotional continuity.

- Many devotionals offer a scripture accompanied by the thoughts and relevant stories of the author. While these are frequently insightful and inspirational, the author's voice is primary. My attention drifts away too easily from the Scripture to the author's thoughts and stories. I want a devotional that keeps the Scripture primary and helps me create space for God to talk to me through the Scripture of the day. I want to listen for what God is saying to me…today…in this Scripture.

- Many devotionals jump around from one favorite scripture to the next. Again, these individual daily devotionals may be inspiring and helpful. However, encountering these scriptures out of context may make it difficult to see the "big picture" of the story of God. I want a devotional that allows me to encounter the Scripture within the larger context in which it is found. When you complete a **40 Days With...** devotional, you will gain a familiarity with the subject of that volume.

Additionally, I want to intentionally reflect on what I'm learning and discerning from my daily encounter with Scripture. For these reasons, my **40 Days With...** devotionals will be both devotional and journal. My hope is that you will find this hybrid approach to devotionals to be a helpful resource in your spiritual life. Every 40 days you can immerse yourself in a fresh scriptural devotional.

ABOUT THE EDITOR

Rev. Chris Barbieri is an ordained Deacon in the United Methodist Church living in Georgia and serving in the North Georgia Conference. Chris is a recognized leader in the area of adult spiritual formation and church leadership. He serves through Digital Deacon Ministries, LLC as an author and consultant. He enjoys leading studies and small groups and his signature workshop is "Better Bible Teaching Starts Now!" Chris also serves on various leadership boards in his community.

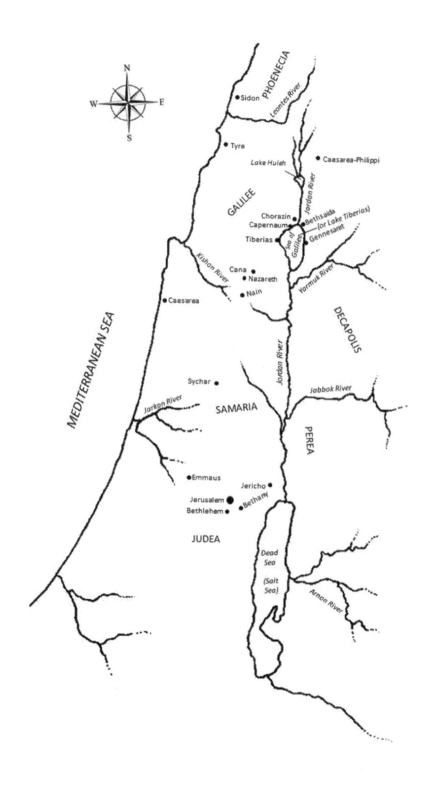

HOW TO USE THIS DEVOTIONAL

Lectio Divina is an ancient practice of the church in which Christians "prayed the scriptures." Individually or in small groups, a passage of scripture was read three or four times – with silence in between each reading. We should remember that very few people could read in the early church and most people encountered scripture by hearing it. Participants listened carefully, not so they could "learn" in an academic sense. Rather, they listened for how God might be speaking to them in that moment. The *40 Days With...* devotionals are designed such that you might listen for God's voice in each day's message in a simi- lar manner.

If you wish to learn more about Lectio Divina, please see my free short eBook *Praying the Scriptures: An Introduction to the History and Practice of Lectio Divina* (currently available on Amazon and Kobo.)

Know that you will likely get what you put into these devotionals. If you hurry through the reading so you can check it off your to-do list, do not expect many insights or spiritual growth.

As with all devotionals, first find a quiet place free of any distractions. Ideally, you will have a regular place for your devotional time. Plan on spending 15-30 minutes on the devotional pages for the day.

1) Pray – Ask God to clear your mind of the mental clutter and invite the Holy Spirit to speak to you.

2) Turn to your current day's devotional pages.

3) Read the passage slowly and carefully.

4) If possible, read it aloud to yourself a second time.

5) First ask yourself if any words or phrases stand out to you. Don't worry about making sense of them. Simply note these words. Each page has a designated space for you to note these words and phrases.

6) Read the passage again (either silently or aloud, as you prefer.)

7) Reflect on the passage in silence. Do you have any insights? How does this passage apply to you...today? Has this passage put something on your "radar?" Has an image popped in your head as you've reflected? Did this passage raise a question in your mind? Do you particularly identify with anyone in the passage? What emotions are present in the passage? What emotions do you feel as you read the passage?

8) Take 5-10 minutes to write down any thoughts you have had during your time of reflection. Each passage has blank space to record your insights, thoughts, and questions.

9) Read the passage one last time. In this final reading, ask yourself if you feel God calling you to any particular action. Record any additional thoughts you may have.

10) Turn back to the front of the devotional and find the index pages. Find the entry for today's passage. In the "Key Phrase" box, write down the main phrase that you focused on from today's passage. In the "Key Insight" box, try to summarize your thoughts on the passage in one or two sentences.

The first few pages of each devotional volume will serve as an index. You will complete the day's index entry AFTER you have completed the daily devotional pages. In the future, the index may help you reference your insights on a particular passage. You may find it beneficial to periodically review the index pages of a completed devotional.

Know that the Bible is more of a library than a single book. It contains many different books by many different authors. Even within the books, different kinds of scripture are encountered. The Gospels contain a mixture of narrative, teaching, and miracle episodes. The Psalms are poetry and Paul's writings are letters.

The narrative sections may not seem as inspiring as one of Jesus' parables, but these sections are important. They connect the story and help us see where Jesus is and to whom he his is speaking. One of the goals of these devotionals is to help you increase your familiarity with your Bible.

On some days you may be overwhelmed with insights about something Jesus taught. You may feel you need more space to write than the devotional provides. On another day, the scripture may tell the story of Jesus moving from point A to point B and you may not discern any major insights. However, knowing that Jesus moved from A to B might inform the next day's reading. Do not worry about how much or little you hear or write on each day. Simply embrace the process of this daily immersion in Scripture.

Why the Common English Bible Translation was Chosen

The Common English Bible (CEB) is the most recent English language scholarly translation of the Bible and was published in 2011. The CEB was a cooperative project involving the Disciples of Christ, Presbyterian Church USA, Episcopal Church, United Church of Christ, and United Methodist Church. Several leading Catholic scholars also participated in this project.

An explicit aim of this project was to produce an easily readable English translation. The editors struck a balance between faithful translation of the original ancient texts and readability.

The CEB is a translation, meaning it originates from ancient texts in their original languages. Many "modern" English Bibles are paraphrases in which the editors may or may not take a good deal of interpretive license in translating passages. While paraphrase Bibles can be useful, I have intentionally chosen an English translation which faithfully adhered to strict standards in translating the original Biblical texts.

I have chosen the CEB because:

1) It is the most current translation. I personally know some of the translation editors who worked on this project and I know it was well done.

2) As the newest English translation, many readers will not be familiar with it. Readers are likely to slow down and pay closer attention as they read the CEB. When we slow down and focus on the Scriptures, we make more room for the Holy Spirit to speak us. My hope is that this relatively fresh translation will let you experience the Bible in a fresh way.

Feel free to use another translation if you would like. For ease of use, I wanted to have everything you needed for quality devotional time in one volume. One of the barriers in my own devotional life is I get frustrated when I'm trying to hold a devotional journal steady, balance a Bible (or smartphone/tablet with a Bible app), and try to write something legible. These devotionals are designed such that all you need is a pen and a quiet place.

More on Translating the Bible

Translating ancient Greek, Hebrew, and Aramaic is not always a straightforward matter. Some passages are notoriously difficult to translate. Also, our modern Bible did not originate as a "single scroll" that was passed down through the centuries. Rather, there are dozens and dozens of scrolls, fragments, and manuscripts that have come down to us through history. These scrolls do not always agree with one another. Determining which version of a passage is most likely the "original" is a challenging scholarly exercise. Early English translators were not aware of many of these challenging translation issues, resulting in noticeable differences in some passages.

For example, there is a "short ending" and a "long ending" to the book of Mark. Most modern scholars agree that the long ending (verses 9-20) was added in the second century. Any good study Bible will point out these finer points of translation in a footnote.

In the CEB, you will occasionally notice a break in sequence between verse numbers. Most of the time, these breaks mean the translation editors believe the missing verses were not a part of the original Biblical text.

USING THIS DEVOTIONAL AS A SMALL GROUP RESOURCE

In addition to using this devotional as a personal study resource, you may wish to use it in a small group setting. You will find it easy to adapt *40 Days with...* books for use as a 6-week resource in a small group. (Your last week will only have 5 days of material.) Two possible formats for this are offered below. Feel free to develop your own format that fits your setting.

Option 1

1) Agree with all study participants on a common start date and ensure everyone has a copy of the devotional.

2) Meet weekly at an agreed upon time and place for 1 hour to 1 hour and 30 minutes.

3) Identify a facilitator and a prayer leader for each week. The prayer leader will open and close the group with prayer. The facilitator will read the scripture and the guiding questions. So that different voices are part of the experience, the facilitator and prayer leader will not be the same person any given week. You may choose to

rotate responsibilities in your group or have one person designated for each role for your small group.

4) You may wish to use this as a template for your sessions:

- Welcome and opening prayer (5 minutes)

- Spend 5-10 minutes on the prior 6 days' of devotional scripture readings. For each, the facilitator should first ask what words or phrases did people note. Then ask if anyone felt called to any particular action or has an insight to share. If anyone felt called to an action, you may wish to ask the person if he/she would like the group to hold him/her accountable. If so, note this and be sure to ask the person about the action in following weeks. (5 minutes per scripture = 30 minutes, 10 minutes per scripture = 60 minutes)

- Spend 20 minutes experiencing the current day's scripture in *Lectio Divina* style.

  □ Begin with 30 seconds of silence for everyone to clear their minds.

  □ The facilitator should read the scripture. Then allow 30 seconds of silence.

  □ Facilitator say: "Hear the scripture again. Listen for words or phrases that catch your attention." Read the scripture again. Allow 30 seconds of silence. Ask participants to note any key words or phrases in the journal section of the book.

  □ Facilitator invites everyone to close their eyes and hear the scripture a third time. Read the scripture again. Allow 15 seconds of silence. Pause 15-20 seconds between each question below.

1. Ask: What emotions are present in the passage?

2. Ask: Did you identify with anyone in particular in the passage?

3. Ask: Did you feel any particular emotions as you heard the passage?

4. Ask: Has an image popped into your mind as you heard the passage?

5. Ask: How does this passage apply to you...today?

▫ Invite participants to take a few minutes to record their thoughts in the journal.

▫ Facilitator say: "Hear the scripture one last time. Do you feel God calling you to some specific action in this passage?" Read the scripture again. Invite people to record any final thoughts.

• Take prayer requests and offer closing prayer (10-15 minutes)

• [Note: You may wish to preview each week's scripture and pre-select one for this *Lectio Divina* experience. It's possible that the group might find one day's scripture more 'interesting' than the seventh day scripture. If you opt for this, be sure to communicate this plan to everyone in your group.]

Option 2

1) Agree with all study participants on a common start date and ensure everyone has a copy of the devotional.

2) Meet weekly at an agreed upon time and place for 1 hour 30 minutes.

3) Rotate responsibility for opening and closing the group with prayer. Use a signup sheet if you wish or simply share the responsibility informally.

4) You may wish to use this as a template for your sessions:

- Welcome and opening prayer (5 minutes)

- Spend approximately 10 minutes on the prior seven days' of devotional scripture readings. For each, the facilitator should first ask what words or phrases did people note. Then ask if anyone felt called to any particular action or has an insight to share. If anyone felt called to an action, you may wish to ask the person if he/she would like the group to hold him/her accountable. If so, note this and be sure to ask the person about the action in following weeks. (10 minutes per scripture = 70 minutes)

- Take prayer requests and offer closing prayer (10-15 minutes)

INTRODUCTION TO THE GOSPEL OF MATTHEW

Matthew's Gospel presents a rich and detailed narrative that presents a complex and multi-dimensional Jesus. This Gospel has two very distinctive features. First, Matthew integrates Jesus with Jewish history and the Jewish scriptural prophecy of the Messiah. Second, the teachings of Jesus are lengthy and explicit when compared to the other Gospels.

The opening genealogy makes it clear from the beginning that a Jewish story is to be told. The flight to Egypt and return to Palestine establishes Jesus and an object of prophecy and serves to connect Jesus with Moses and memories of the Exodus. Throughout Matthew, events in the story of Jesus are explicitly linked to Jewish prophecy about the Messiah. These connections build the case of Jesus as Messiah and the central theme of Matthew is the revelation of Jesus as the long-foretold Messiah.

Unlike Mark, the teachings of Jesus take precedence over miracles in Matthew. In fact, the first miracle does not occur until chapter 8 in Matthew. Matthew is notable for five long teaching sections, with the Sermon on the Mount being the most famous of these (Matthew 5:1 – 7:27.) The story shifts from narrative to monologue during these long teachings and Matthew takes on a first-person quality for long stretches. These teaching discourses form the spine of Matthew. The *story* of Jesus comes to a halt and the *teaching* of Jesus the Messiah dominates. Narrative episodes serve to link Jesus with prophetic scripture, provide a righteous example to the disciples, or demonstrate his power and authority through miracles. The Passion and Easter stories form a powerful conclusion that fuses the roles of Jesus the teacher with Jesus the Messiah together.

40 Days with the Gospel of Matthew, Vol 1. follows Jesus from birth through the majority of his Galilean ministry. The second volume begins in Galilee as Jesus begins to foretell of his death and then follows Jesus to Jerusalem and ultimately the cross and empty tomb.

Also Noteworthy:

The ancient manuscripts of Matthew are written in a more polished form of Greek than Mark. Some early church traditions say it was originally written in Aramaic, but there is no concrete evidence of this. It should be noted how unlikely it is that the disciple Matthew would have been able to write in literary Greek.

Joseph is the central figure in the birth story, not Mary. Some have suggested the references to dreams are a possible link to the Old Testament figure of Joseph. Matthew mentions no Roman census like Luke and the family is already living in Bethlehem. In general, Matthew and Luke have significant differences concerning the birth of Jesus.

While the Gospel of Matthew tells of the call of Peter, Andrew, James, John, and Matthew, it is unclear when the rest of the disciples were called. Matthew is not introduced until 9:9, which raises the question as to whether any disciples but the original four were present for the Sermon on the Mount.

This Gospel also features Jesus making a number of references to the "Law" and there is considerable usage of symbolic numbers (3's, 5's, and 7's). Those who call Jesus 'teacher' in Matthew frequently fail to recognize him as the Son of God. Matthew is also the only gospel to use the word church (Greek: *ekklesia*).

Devotional Start Date: _____

Day 1	Matthew 1:1-17	Key phrase

Key Insight

Day 2	Matthew 1:18-25	Key phrase

Key Insight

Day 3	Matthew 2:1-15	Key phrase

Key Insight

Day 4	Matthew 2:16-23	Key phrase

Key Insight

Day 5	Matthew 3:1-12	Key phrase

Key Insight

40 Days With...

Day 6	Matthew 3:13–4:11	Key phrase

Key Insight

Day 7	Matthew 4:12-22	Key phrase

Key Insight

Day 8	Matthew 4:23-5:12	Key phrase

Key Insight

Day 9	Matthew 5:13-20	Key phrase

Key Insight

Day 10	Matthew 5:21-26	Key phrase

Key Insight

Day 11	Matthew 5:27-37	Key phrase

Key Insight

Day 12	Matthew 5:38-48	Key phrase

Key Insight

Day 13	Matthew 6:1-15	Key phrase

Key Insight

Day 14	Matthew 6:16-24	Key phrase

Key Insight

Day 15	Matthew 6:25-34	Key phrase

Key Insight

Day 16	Matthew 7:1-12	Key phrase

Key Insight

Day 17	Matthew 7:13-23	Key phrase

Key Insight

Day 18	Matthew 7:24–8:4	Key phrase

Key Insight

Day 19	Matthew 8:5-13	Key phrase

Key Insight

Day 20	Matthew 8:14-22	Key phrase

Key Insight

Day 21	Matthew 8:23-27	Key phrase

Key Insight

Day 22	Matthew 8:28-34	Key phrase

Key Insight

Day 23	Matthew 9:1-8	Key phrase

Key Insight

Day 24	Matthew 9:9-17	Key phrase

Key Insight

Day 25	Matthew 9:18-26	Key phrase

Key Insight

Day 26	Matthew 9:27-38	Key phrase

Key Insight

Day 27	Matthew 10:1-15	Key phrase

Key Insight

Day 28	Matthew 10:26-33	Key phrase

Key Insight

Day 29	Matthew 10:34-42	Key phrase

Key Insight

Day 30	Matthew 11:2-15	Key phrase

Key Insight

Day 31	Matthew 12:1-14	Key phrase
Key Insight		

Day 32	Matthew 12:22-32	Key phrase
Key Insight		

Day 33	Matthew 13:1-9, 18-23	Key phrase
Key Insight		

Day 34	Matthew 13:10-17, 31-35	Key phrase
Key Insight		

Day 35	Matthew 13:24-30, 36-43	Key phrase
Key Insight		

Day 36	Matthew 13:44-53	Key phrase

Key Insight

Day 37	Matthew 13:54–14:12	Key phrase

Key Insight

Day 38	Matthew 14:13-21	Key phrase

Key Insight

Day 39	Matthew 14:22-33	Key phrase

Key Insight

Day 40	Matthew 15:1-20	Key phrase

Key Insight

ONE FINAL THOUGHT...

If you are familiar with the day's passage, avoid the trap of rushing through it. I believe the Holy Spirit speaks to us through Scripture if we allow the proper time and space. Too often when we encounter a familiar Scripture, we allow our minds to rush to the end ("Oh yeah... know how this parable ends"). Our minds turn away from Scripture to our normal mental clutter. As you progress through the devotional, avoid this trap and listen carefully to what the Scripture is saying to you today. Try to erase any preconceptions about the passage and approach it with fresh eyes and ears. I have found this practice to be incredibly fruitful in my own personal study. I notice things I never noticed before and I hear things I've missed over and over in prior readings.

Matthew 1:1-17

1   A record of the ancestors of Jesus Christ, son of David, son of Abraham:

2   Abraham was the father of Isaac. Isaac was the father of Jacob. Jacob was the father of Judah and his brothers.

3   Judah was the father of Perez and Zerah, whose mother was Tamar. Perez was the father of Hezron. Hezron was the father of Aram.

4   Aram was the father of Amminadab. Amminadab was the father of Nahshon. Nahshon was the father of Salmon.

5   Salmon was the father of Boaz, whose mother was Rahab. Boaz was the father of Obed, whose mother was Ruth. Obed was the father of Jesse.

6   Jesse was the father of David the king. David was the father of Solomon, whose mother had been the wife of Uriah.

7   Solomon was the father of Rehoboam. Rehoboam was the father of Abijah. Abijah was the father of Asaph.

8   Asaph was the father of Jehoshaphat. Jehoshaphat was the father of Joram. Joram was the father of Uzziah.

9   Uzziah was the father of Jotham. Jotham was the father of Ahaz. Ahaz was the father of Hezekiah.

10 Hezekiah was the father of Manasseh. Manasseh was the father of Amos. Amos was the father of Josiah.

11   Josiah was the father of Jechoniah and his brothers. This was at the time of the exile to Babylon.

12   After the exile to Babylon: Jechoniah was the father of Shealtiel. Shealtiel was the father of Zerubbabel.

13   Zerubbabel was the father of Abiud. Abiud was the father of Eliakim. Eliakim was the father of Azor.

14   Azor was the father of Zadok. Zadok was the father of Achim. Achim was the father of Eliud.

15   Eliud was the father of Eleazar. Eleazar was the father of Matthan. Matthan was the father of Jacob.

16   Jacob was the father of Joseph, the husband of Mary—of whom Jesus was born, who is called the Christ.

17   So there were fourteen generations from Abraham to David, fourteen generations from David to the exile to Babylon, and fourteen generations from the exile to Babylon to the Christ.

Key words or phrases?

Insights?

Matthew 1:18-25

18 This is how the birth of Jesus Christ took place. When Mary his mother was engaged to Joseph, before they were married, she became pregnant by the Holy Spirit.

19 Joseph her husband was a righteous man. Because he didn't want to humiliate her, he decided to call off their engagement quietly.

20 As he was thinking about this, an angel from the Lord appeared to him in a dream and said, "Joseph son of David, don't be afraid to take Mary as your wife, because the child she carries was conceived by the Holy Spirit.

21 She will give birth to a son, and you will call him Jesus, because he will save his people from their sins."

22 Now all of this took place so that what the Lord had spoken through the prophet would be fulfilled:

23   Look! A virgin will become pregnant and give birth
        to a son,
            And they will call him, Emmanuel.
        (Emmanuel means "God with us.")

24 When Joseph woke up, he did just as an angel from God commanded and took Mary as his wife.

25 But he didn't have sexual relations with her until she gave birth to a son. Joseph called him Jesus.

Key words or phrases?

Insights?

Matthew 2:1-15

¹ After Jesus was born in Bethlehem in the territory of Judea during the rule of King Herod, magi came from the east to Jerusalem.

² They asked, "Where is the newborn king of the Jews? We've seen his star in the east, and we've come to honor him."

³ When King Herod heard this, he was troubled, and everyone in Jerusalem was troubled with him.

⁴ He gathered all the chief priests and the legal experts and asked them where the Christ was to be born.

⁵ They said, "In Bethlehem of Judea, for this is what the prophet wrote:

⁶ You, Bethlehem, land of Judah,
by no means are you least among the rulers of Judah,
because from you will come one who governs,
who will shepherd my people Israel."

⁷ Then Herod secretly called for the magi and found out from them the time when the star had first appeared.

⁸ He sent them to Bethlehem, saying, "Go and search carefully for the child. When you've found him, report to me so that I too may go and honor him."

⁹ When they heard the king, they went; and look, the star they had seen in the east went ahead of them until it stood over the place where the child was.

10   When they saw the star, they were filled with joy.

11   They entered the house and saw the child with Mary his mother. Falling to their knees, they honored him. Then they opened their treasure chests and presented him with gifts of gold, frankincense, and myrrh.

12   Because they were warned in a dream not to return to Herod, they went back to their own country by another route.

13   When the magi had departed, an angel from the Lord appeared to Joseph in a dream and said, "Get up. Take the child and his mother and escape to Egypt. Stay there until I tell you, for Herod will soon search for the child in order to kill him."

14   Joseph got up and, during the night, took the child and his mother to Egypt.

15   He stayed there until Herod died. This fulfilled what the Lord had spoken through the prophet: I have called my son out of Egypt.

Key words or phrases?

Insights?

Matthew 2:16-23

16   When Herod knew the magi had fooled him, he grew very angry. He sent soldiers to kill all the children in Bethlehem and in all the surrounding territory who were two years old and younger, according to the time that he had learned from the magi.

17   This fulfilled the word spoken through Jeremiah the prophet:

18   A voice was heard in Ramah,
      weeping and much grieving.
        Rachel weeping for her children,
      and she did not want to be comforted,
      because they were no more.

19   After King Herod died, an angel from the Lord appeared in a dream to Joseph in Egypt.

20   "Get up," the angel said, "and take the child and his mother and go to the land of Israel. Those who were trying to kill the child are dead."

21   Joseph got up, took the child and his mother, and went to the land of Israel.

22   But when he heard that Archelaus ruled over Judea in place of his father Herod, Joseph was afraid to go there. Having been warned in a dream, he went to the area of Galilee.

23   He settled in a city called Nazareth so that what was spoken through the prophets might be fulfilled: He will be called a Nazarene.

Key words or phrases?

Insights?

Matthew 3:1-12

1 In those days John the Baptist appeared in the desert of Judea announcing, 2 "Change your hearts and lives! Here comes the kingdom of heaven!"

3 He was the one of whom Isaiah the prophet spoke when he said:

> The voice of one shouting in the wilderness,
> "Prepare the way for the Lord;
> make his paths straight."

4 John wore clothes made of camel's hair, with a leather belt around his waist. He ate locusts and wild honey.

5 People from Jerusalem, throughout Judea, and all around the Jordan River came to him.

6 As they confessed their sins, he baptized them in the Jordan River.

7 Many Pharisees and Sadducees came to be baptized by John. He said to them, "You children of snakes! Who warned you to escape from the angry judgment that is coming soon?

8 Produce fruit that shows you have changed your hearts and lives.

9 And don't even think about saying to yourselves, Abraham is our father. I tell you that God is able to raise up Abraham's children from these stones.

10 The ax is already at the root of the trees. Therefore, every tree

that doesn't produce good fruit will be chopped down and tossed into the fire.

11 I baptize with water those of you who have changed your hearts and lives. The one who is coming after me is stronger than I am. I'm not worthy to carry his sandals. He will baptize you with the Holy Spirit and with fire.

12 The shovel he uses to sift the wheat from the husks is in his hands. He will clean out his threshing area and bring the wheat into his barn. But he will burn the husks with a fire that can't be put out."

Key words or phrases?

Insights?

Matthew 3:13–4:11

13 At that time Jesus came from Galilee to the Jordan River so that John would baptize him.

14 John tried to stop him and said, "I need to be baptized by you, yet you come to me?"

15 Jesus answered, "Allow me to be baptized now. This is necessary to fulfill all righteousness." So John agreed to baptize Jesus.

16 When Jesus was baptized, he immediately came up out of the water. Heaven was opened to him, and he saw the Spirit of God coming down like a dove and resting on him.

17 A voice from heaven said, "This is my Son whom I dearly love; I find happiness in him."

1 Then the Spirit led Jesus up into the wilderness so that the devil might tempt him.

2 After Jesus had fasted for forty days and forty nights, he was starving.

3 The tempter came to him and said, "Since you are God's Son, command these stones to become bread."

4 Jesus replied, "It's written, People won't live only by bread, but by every word spoken by God."

5 After that the devil brought him into the holy city and stood him at the highest point of the temple. He said to him,

6   "Since you are God's Son, throw yourself down; for it is written, I will command my angels concerning you, and they will take you up in their hands so that you won't hit your foot on a stone."

7   Jesus replied, "Again it's written, Don't test the Lord your God."

8   Then the devil brought him to a very high mountain and showed him all the kingdoms of the world and their glory.

9   He said, "I'll give you all these if you bow down and worship me."

10 Jesus responded, "Go away, Satan, because it's written, You will worship the Lord your God and serve only him."

11 The devil left him, and angels came and took care of him.

Key words or phrases?

Insights?

Matthew 4:12-22

12 Now when Jesus heard that John was arrested, he went to Galilee.

13 He left Nazareth and settled in Capernaum, which lies alongside the sea in the area of Zebulun and Naphtali.

14 This fulfilled what Isaiah the prophet said:

15 Land of Zebulun and land of Naphtali,
alongside the sea, across the Jordan, Galilee of the Gentiles,
16 the people who lived in the dark have seen a great light,
and a light has come upon those who lived in the region
and in shadow of death.

17 From that time Jesus began to announce, "Change your hearts and lives! Here comes the kingdom of heaven!"

18 As Jesus walked alongside the Galilee Sea, he saw two brothers, Simon, who is called Peter, and Andrew, throwing fishing nets into the sea, because they were fishermen.

19 "Come, follow me," he said, "and I'll show you how to fish for people."

20 Right away, they left their nets and followed him.

21 Continuing on, he saw another set of brothers, James the son of Zebedee and his brother John. They were in a boat with Zebedee their father repairing their nets. Jesus called them and 22 immediately they left the boat and their father and followed him.

Key words or phrases?

Insights?

Matthew 4:23-5:12

23 Jesus traveled throughout Galilee, teaching in their synagogues. He announced the good news of the kingdom and healed every disease and sickness among the people.

24 News about him spread throughout Syria. People brought to him all those who had various kinds of diseases, those in pain, those possessed by demons, those with epilepsy, and those who were paralyzed, and he healed them.

25 Large crowds followed him from Galilee, the Decapolis, Jerusalem, Judea, and from the areas beyond the Jordan River.

1 Now when Jesus saw the crowds, he went up a mountain. He sat down and his disciples came to him.

2 He taught them, saying:

3 "Happy are people who are hopeless, because the kingdom of heaven is theirs.

4 "Happy are people who grieve, because they will be made glad.

5 "Happy are people who are humble, because they will inherit the earth.

6 "Happy are people who are hungry and thirsty for righteousness, because they will be fed until they are full.

7 "Happy are people who show mercy, because they will receive mercy.

8   "Happy are people who have pure hearts, because they will see God.

9   "Happy are people who make peace, because they will be called God's children.

10   "Happy are people whose lives are harassed because they are righteous, because the kingdom of heaven is theirs.

11   "Happy are you when people insult you and harass you and speak all kinds of bad and false things about you, all because of me.

12   Be full of joy and be glad, because you have a great reward in heaven. In the same way, people harassed the prophets who came before you.

Key words or phrases?

Insights?

Matthew 5:13-20

13 "You are the salt of the earth; but if salt has lost its taste, how can its saltiness be restored? It is no longer good for anything, but is thrown out and trampled under foot.

14 "You are the light of the world. A city built on a hill cannot be hid.

15 No one after lighting a lamp puts it under the bushel basket, but on the lampstand, and it gives light to all in the house.

16 In the same way, let your light shine before others, so that they may see your good works and give glory to your Father in heaven.

17 "Do not think that I have come to abolish the law or the prophets; I have come not to abolish but to fulfill.

18 For truly I tell you, until heaven and earth pass away, not one letter, not one stroke of a letter, will pass from the law until all is accomplished.

19 Therefore, whoever breaks one of the least of these commandments, and teaches others to do the same, will be called least in the kingdom of heaven; but whoever does them and teaches them will be called great in the kingdom of heaven.

20 For I tell you, unless your righteousness exceeds that of the scribes and Pharisees, you will never enter the kingdom of heaven.

Key words or phrases?

Insights?

Matthew 5:21-26

21 "You have heard that it was said to those who lived long ago, Don't commit murder, and all who commit murder will be in danger of judgment.

22 But I say to you that everyone who is angry with their brother or sister will be in danger of judgment. If they say to their brother or sister, 'You idiot,' they will be in danger of being condemned by the governing council. And if they say, 'You fool,' they will be in danger of fiery hell.

23 Therefore, if you bring your gift to the altar and there remember that your brother or sister has something against you, 24 leave your gift at the altar and go. First make things right with your brother or sister and then come back and offer your gift.

25 Be sure to make friends quickly with your opponents while you are with them on the way to court. Otherwise, they will haul you before the judge, the judge will turn you over to the officer of the court, and you will be thrown into prison.

26 I say to you in all seriousness that you won't get out of there until you've paid the very last penny.

Key words or phrases?

Insights?

Matthew 5:27-37

27 "You have heard that it was said, Don't commit adultery.

28 But I say to you that every man who looks at a woman lustfully has already committed adultery in his heart.

29 And if your right eye causes you to fall into sin, tear it out and throw it away. It's better that you lose a part of your body than that your whole body be thrown into hell.

30 And if your right hand causes you to fall into sin, chop it off and throw it away. It's better that you lose a part of your body than that your whole body go into hell.

31 "It was said, 'Whoever divorces his wife must give her a divorce certificate.'

32 But I say to you that whoever divorces his wife except for sexual unfaithfulness forces her to commit adultery. And whoever marries a divorced woman commits adultery.

33 "Again you have heard that it was said to those who lived long ago: Don't make a false solemn pledge, but you should follow through on what you have pledged to the Lord.

34 But I say to you that you must not pledge at all. You must not pledge by heaven, because it's God's throne.

35 You must not pledge by the earth, because it's God's footstool. You must not pledge by Jerusalem, because it's the city of the great king.

36 And you must not pledge by your head, because you can't turn one hair white or black.

37 Let your yes mean yes, and your no mean no. Anything more than this comes from the evil one.

Key words or phrases?

Insights?

Matthew 5:38-48

38 "You have heard that it was said, An eye for an eye and a tooth for a tooth.

39 But I say to you that you must not oppose those who want to hurt you. If people slap you on your right cheek, you must turn the left cheek to them as well.

40 When they wish to haul you to court and take your shirt, let them have your coat too.

41 When they force you to go one mile, go with them two.

42 Give to those who ask, and don't refuse those who wish to borrow from you.

43 "You have heard that it was said, You must love your neighbor and hate your enemy.

44 But I say to you, love your enemies and pray for those who harass you 45 so that you will be acting as children of your Father who is in heaven. He makes the sun rise on both the evil and the good and sends rain on both the righteous and the unrighteous.

46 If you love only those who love you, what reward do you have? Don't even the tax collectors do the same?

47 And if you greet only your brothers and sisters, what more are you doing? Don't even the Gentiles do the same?

48 Therefore, just as your heavenly Father is complete in showing love to everyone, so also you must be complete.

Key words or phrases?

Insights?

Matthew 6:1-15

1 "Be careful that you don't practice your religion in front of people to draw their attention. If you do, you will have no reward from your Father who is in heaven.

2 "Whenever you give to the poor, don't blow your trumpet as the hypocrites do in the synagogues and in the streets so that they may get praise from people. I assure you, that's the only reward they'll get.

3 But when you give to the poor, don't let your left hand know what your right hand is doing 4 so that you may give to the poor in secret. Your Father who sees what you do in secret will reward you.

5 "When you pray, don't be like hypocrites. They love to pray standing in the synagogues and on the street corners so that people will see them. I assure you, that's the only reward they'll get.

6 But when you pray, go to your room, shut the door, and pray to your Father who is present in that secret place. Your Father who sees what you do in secret will reward you.

7 "When you pray, don't pour out a flood of empty words, as the Gentiles do. They think that by saying many words they'll be heard.

8 Don't be like them, because your Father knows what you need before you ask.

⁹ Pray like this:

> Our Father who is in heaven,
> uphold the holiness of your name.
¹⁰ > Bring in your kingdom
> so that your will is done on earth as it's done in heaven.
¹¹ > Give us the bread we need for today.
¹² > Forgive us for the ways we have wronged you,
> just as we also forgive those who have wronged us.
¹³ > And don't lead us into temptation,
> but rescue us from the evil one.

¹⁴ "If you forgive others their sins, your heavenly Father will also forgive you.

¹⁵ But if you don't forgive others, neither will your Father forgive your sins.

Key words or phrases?

Insights?

Matthew 6:16-24

16   "And when you fast, don't put on a sad face like the hypocrites. They distort their faces so people will know they are fasting. I assure you that they have their reward.

17   When you fast, brush your hair and wash your face.

18   Then you won't look like you are fasting to people, but only to your Father who is present in that secret place. Your Father who sees in secret will reward you.

19   "Stop collecting treasures for your own benefit on earth, where moth and rust eat them and where thieves break in and steal them.

20   Instead, collect treasures for yourselves in heaven, where moth and rust don't eat them and where thieves don't break in and steal them.

21   Where your treasure is, there your heart will be also.

22   "The eye is the lamp of the body. Therefore, if your eye is healthy, your whole body will be full of light.

23   But if your eye is bad, your whole body will be full of darkness. If then the light in you is darkness, how terrible that darkness will be!

24   No one can serve two masters. Either you will hate the one and love the other, or you will be loyal to the one and have contempt for the other. You cannot serve God and wealth.

Key words or phrases?

Insights?

Matthew 6:25-34

25   "Therefore, I say to you, don't worry about your life, what you'll eat or what you'll drink, or about your body, what you'll wear. Isn't life more than food and the body more than clothes?

26   Look at the birds in the sky. They don't sow seed or harvest grain or gather crops into barns. Yet your heavenly Father feeds them. Aren't you worth much more than they are?

27   Who among you by worrying can add a single moment to your life?

28   And why do you worry about clothes? Notice how the lilies in the field grow. They don't wear themselves out with work, and they don't spin cloth.

29   But I say to you that even Solomon in all of his splendor wasn't dressed like one of these.

30   If God dresses grass in the field so beautifully, even though it's alive today and tomorrow it's thrown into the furnace, won't God do much more for you, you people of weak faith?

31   Therefore, don't worry and say, 'What are we going to eat?' or 'What are we going to drink?' or 'What are we going to wear?'

32   Gentiles long for all these things. Your heavenly Father knows that you need them.

33   Instead, desire first and foremost God's kingdom and God's righteousness, and all these things will be given to you as well.

34   Therefore, stop worrying about tomorrow, because tomorrow will worry about itself. Each day has enough trouble of its own.

Key words or phrases?

Insights?

Matthew 7:1-12

1   "Don't judge, so that you won't be judged.

2   You'll receive the same judgment you give. Whatever you deal out will be dealt out to you.

3   Why do you see the splinter that's in your brother's or sister's eye, but don't notice the log in your own eye?

4   How can you say to your brother or sister, 'Let me take the splinter out of your eye,' when there's a log in your eye?

5   You deceive yourself! First take the log out of your eye, and then you'll see clearly to take the splinter out of your brother's or sister's eye.

6   Don't give holy things to dogs, and don't throw your pearls in front of pigs. They will stomp on the pearls, then turn around and attack you.

7   "Ask, and you will receive. Search, and you will find. Knock, and the door will be opened to you.

8   For everyone who asks, receives. Whoever seeks, finds. And to everyone who knocks, the door is opened.

9   Who among you will give your children a stone when they ask for bread?

10   Or give them a snake when they ask for fish?

11   If you who are evil know how to give good gifts to your children, how much more will your heavenly Father give good things to those who ask him.

12   Therefore, you should treat people in the same way that you want people to treat you; this is the Law and the Prophets.

Key words or phrases?

Insights?

Matthew 7:13-23

13 "Go in through the narrow gate. The gate that leads to destruction is broad and the road wide, so many people enter through it.

14 But the gate that leads to life is narrow and the road difficult, so few people find it.

15 "Watch out for false prophets. They come to you dressed like sheep, but inside they are vicious wolves.

16 You will know them by their fruit. Do people get bunches of grapes from thorny weeds, or do they get figs from thistles?

17 In the same way, every good tree produces good fruit, and every rotten tree produces bad fruit.

18 A good tree can't produce bad fruit. And a rotten tree can't produce good fruit.

19 Every tree that doesn't produce good fruit is chopped down and thrown into the fire.

20 Therefore, you will know them by their fruit.

21 "Not everybody who says to me, 'Lord, Lord,' will get into the kingdom of heaven. Only those who do the will of my Father who is in heaven will enter.

22 On the Judgment Day, many people will say to me, 'Lord, Lord, didn't we prophesy in your name and expel demons in your name and do lots of miracles in your name?'

23 Then I'll tell them, 'I've never known you. Get away from me, you people who do wrong.'

Key words or phrases?

Insights?

Matthew 7:24–8:4

24 "Everybody who hears these words of mine and puts them into practice is like a wise builder who built a house on bedrock.

25 The rain fell, the floods came, and the wind blew and beat against that house. It didn't fall because it was firmly set on bedrock.

26 But everybody who hears these words of mine and doesn't put them into practice will be like a fool who built a house on sand.

27 The rain fell, the floods came, and the wind blew and beat against that house. It fell and was completely destroyed."

28 When Jesus finished these words, the crowds were amazed at his teaching 29 because he was teaching them like someone with authority and not like their legal experts.

1 Now when Jesus had come down from the mountain, large crowds followed him.

2 A man with a skin disease came, kneeled before him, and said, "Lord, if you want, you can make me clean."

3 Jesus reached out his hand and touched him, saying, "I do want to. Become clean." Instantly his skin disease was cleansed.

4 Jesus said to him, "Don't say anything to anyone. Instead, go and show yourself to the priest and offer the gift that Moses commanded. This will be a testimony to them."

Key words or phrases?

Insights?

Matthew 8:5-13

5 When Jesus went to Capernaum, a centurion approached, 6 pleading with him, "Lord, my servant is flat on his back at home, paralyzed, and his suffering is awful."

7 Jesus responded, "I'll come and heal him."

8 But the centurion replied, "Lord, I don't deserve to have you come under my roof. Just say the word and my servant will be healed.

9 I'm a man under authority, with soldiers under me. I say to one, 'Go,' and he goes, and to another, 'Come,' and he comes. I say to my servant, 'Do this,' and the servant does it."

10 When Jesus heard this, he was impressed and said to the people following him, "I say to you with all seriousness that even in Israel I haven't found faith like this.

11 I say to you that there are many who will come from east and west and sit down to eat with Abraham and Isaac and Jacob in the kingdom of heaven.

12 But the children of the kingdom will be thrown outside into the darkness. People there will be weeping and grinding their teeth."

13 Jesus said to the centurion, "Go; it will be done for you just as you have believed." And his servant was healed that very moment.

Key words or phrases?

Insights?

Matthew 8:14-22

14 Jesus went home with Peter and saw Peter's mother-in-law lying in bed with a fever.

15 He touched her hand, and the fever left her. Then she got up and served them.

16 That evening people brought to Jesus many who were demon-possessed. He threw the spirits out with just a word. He healed everyone who was sick.

17 This happened so that what Isaiah the prophet said would be fulfilled: He is the one who took our illnesses and carried away our diseases.

18 Now when Jesus saw the crowd, he ordered his disciples to go over to the other side of the lake.

19 A legal expert came and said to him, "Teacher, I'll follow you wherever you go."

20 Jesus replied, "Foxes have dens, and the birds in the sky have nests, but the Human One has no place to lay his head."

21 Another man, one of his disciples, said to him, "Lord, first let me go and bury my father."

22 But Jesus said to him, "Follow me, and let the dead bury their own dead.

Key words or phrases?

Insights?

Matthew 8:23-27

23 When Jesus got into a boat, his disciples followed him.

24 A huge storm arose on the lake so that waves were sloshing over the boat. But Jesus was asleep.

25 They came and woke him, saying, "Lord, rescue us! We're going to drown!"

26 He said to them, "Why are you afraid, you people of weak faith?" Then he got up and gave orders to the winds and the lake, and there was a great calm.

27 The people were amazed and said, "What kind of person is this? Even the winds and the lake obey him!"

Key words or phrases?

Insights?

Matthew 8:28-34

28 When Jesus arrived on the other side of the lake in the country of the Gadarenes, two men who were demon-possessed came from among the tombs to meet him. They were so violent that nobody could travel on that road.

29 They cried out, "What are you going to do with us, Son of God? Have you come to torture us before the time of judgment?"

30 Far off in the distance a large herd of pigs was feeding.

31 The demons pleaded with him, "If you throw us out, send us into the herd of pigs."

32 Then he said to the demons, "Go away," and they came out and went into the pigs. The whole herd rushed down the cliff into the lake and drowned.

33 Those who tended the pigs ran into the city and told everything that had happened to the demon-possessed men.

34 Then the whole city came out and met Jesus. When they saw him, they pleaded with him to leave their region.

Key words or phrases?

Insights?

Matthew 9:1-8

1 Boarding a boat, Jesus crossed to the other side of the lake and went to his own city.

2 People brought to him a man who was paralyzed, lying on a cot. When Jesus saw their faith, he said to the man who was paralyzed, "Be encouraged, my child, your sins are forgiven."

3 Some legal experts said among themselves, "This man is insulting God."

4 But Jesus knew what they were thinking and said, "Why do you fill your minds with evil things?

5 Which is easier—to say, 'Your sins are forgiven,' or to say, 'Get up and walk'?

6 But so you will know that the Human One has authority on the earth to forgive sins"—he said to the man who was paralyzed—"Get up, take your cot, and go home."

7 The man got up and went home.

8 When the crowds saw what had happened, they were afraid and praised God, who had given such authority to human beings.

Key words or phrases?

Insights?

Matthew 9:9-17

9   As Jesus continued on from there, he saw a man named Matthew sitting at a kiosk for collecting taxes. He said to him, "Follow me," and he got up and followed him.

10   As Jesus sat down to eat in Matthew's house, many tax collectors and sinners joined Jesus and his disciples at the table.

11   But when the Pharisees saw this, they said to his disciples, "Why does your teacher eat with tax collectors and sinners?"

12   When Jesus heard it, he said, "Healthy people don't need a doctor, but sick people do.

13   Go and learn what this means: I want mercy and not sacrifice. I didn't come to call righteous people, but sinners."

14   At that time John's disciples came and asked Jesus, "Why do we and the Pharisees frequently fast, but your disciples never fast?"

15   Jesus responded, "The wedding guests can't mourn while the groom is still with them, can they? But the days will come when the groom will be taken away from them, and then they'll fast.

16   "No one sews a piece of new, unshrunk cloth on old clothes because the patch tears away the cloth and makes a worse tear.

17   No one pours new wine into old wineskins. If they did, the wineskins would burst, the wine would spill, and the wineskins would be ruined. Instead, people pour new wine into new wineskins so that both are kept safe."

Key words or phrases?

Insights?

Matthew 9:18-26

18 While Jesus was speaking to them, a ruler came and knelt in front of him, saying, "My daughter has just died. But come and place your hand on her, and she'll live."

19 So Jesus and his disciples got up and went with him.

20 Then a woman who had been bleeding for twelve years came up behind Jesus and touched the hem of his clothes.

21 She thought, if I only touch his robe I'll be healed.

22 When Jesus turned and saw her, he said, "Be encouraged, daughter. Your faith has healed you." And the woman was healed from that time on.

23 When Jesus went into the ruler's house, he saw the flute players and the distressed crowd.

24 He said, "Go away, because the little girl isn't dead but is asleep"; but they laughed at him.

25 After he had sent the crowd away, Jesus went in and touched her hand, and the little girl rose up.

26 News about this spread throughout that whole region.

Key words or phrases?

Insights?

Matthew 9:27-38

27 As Jesus departed, two blind men followed him, crying out, "Show us mercy, Son of David."

28 When he came into the house, the blind men approached him. Jesus said to them, "Do you believe I can do this?"

"Yes, Lord," they replied.

29 Then Jesus touched their eyes and said, "It will happen for you just as you have believed."

30 Their eyes were opened. Then Jesus sternly warned them, "Make sure nobody knows about this."

31 But they went out and spread the word about him throughout that whole region.

32 As they were leaving, people brought to him a man who was demon-possessed and unable to speak.

33 When Jesus had thrown out the demon, the man who couldn't speak began to talk. The crowds were amazed and said, "Nothing like this has ever been seen in Israel."

34 But the Pharisees said, "He throws out demons with the authority of the ruler of demons."

35 Jesus traveled among all the cities and villages, teaching in their synagogues, announcing the good news of the kingdom, and healing every disease and every sickness.

36 Now when Jesus saw the crowds, he had compassion for them because they were troubled and helpless, like sheep without a shepherd.

37 Then he said to his disciples, "The size of the harvest is bigger than you can imagine, but there are few workers.

38 Therefore, plead with the Lord of the harvest to send out workers for his harvest."

Key words or phrases?

Insights?

Matthew 10:1-15

1   He called his twelve disciples and gave them authority over unclean spirits to throw them out and to heal every disease and every sickness.

2   Here are the names of the twelve apostles: first, Simon, who is called Peter; and Andrew his brother; James the son of Zebedee; and John his brother; ³ Philip; and Bartholomew; Thomas; and Matthew the tax collector; James the son of Alphaeus; and Thaddaeus; ⁴ Simon the Cananaean; and Judas, who betrayed Jesus.

5   Jesus sent these twelve out and commanded them, "Don't go among the Gentiles or into a Samaritan city.

6   Go instead to the lost sheep, the people of Israel.

7   As you go, make this announcement: 'The kingdom of heaven has come near.'

8   Heal the sick, raise the dead, cleanse those with skin diseases, and throw out demons. You received without having to pay. Therefore, give without demanding payment.

9   Workers deserve to be fed, so don't gather gold or silver or copper coins for your money belts to take on your trips.

10 Don't take a backpack for the road or two shirts or sandals or a walking stick.

11 Whatever city or village you go into, find somebody in it who is worthy and stay there until you go on your way.

12   When you go into a house, say, 'Peace!'

13   If the house is worthy, give it your blessing of peace. But if the house isn't worthy, take back your blessing.

14   If anyone refuses to welcome you or listen to your words, shake the dust off your feet as you leave that house or city.

15   I assure you that it will be more bearable for the land of Sodom and Gomorrah on Judgment Day than it will be for that city.

Matthew 10:26-33

26   "Therefore, don't be afraid of those people because nothing is hidden that won't be revealed, and nothing secret that won't be brought out into the open.

27   What I say to you in the darkness, tell in the light; and what you hear whispered, announce from the rooftops.

28   Don't be afraid of those who kill the body but can't kill the soul. Instead, be afraid of the one who can destroy both body and soul in hell.

29   Aren't two sparrows sold for a small coin? But not one of them will fall to the ground without your Father knowing about it already.

30   Even the hairs of your head are all counted.

31   Don't be afraid. You are worth more than many sparrows.

32   "Therefore, everyone who acknowledges me before people, I also will acknowledge before my Father who is in heaven.

33   But everyone who denies me before people, I also will deny before my Father who is in heaven.

Key words or phrases?

Insights?

Matthew 10:34-42

34 "Don't think that I've come to bring peace to the earth. I haven't come to bring peace but a sword.

35 I've come to turn a man against his father, a daughter against her mother, and a daughter-in-law against her mother-in-law.

36 People's enemies are members of their own households.

37 "Those who love father or mother more than me aren't worthy of me. Those who love son or daughter more than me aren't worthy of me.

38 Those who don't pick up their crosses and follow me aren't worthy of me.

39 Those who find their lives will lose them, and those who lose their lives because of me will find them.

40 "Those who receive you are also receiving me, and those who receive me are receiving the one who sent me.

41 Those who receive a prophet as a prophet will receive a prophet's reward. Those who receive a righteous person as a righteous person will receive a righteous person's reward.

42 I assure you that everybody who gives even a cup of cold water to these little ones because they are my disciples will certainly be rewarded."

Key words or phrases?

Insights?

Matthew 11:2-15

2 Now when John heard in prison about the things the Christ was doing, he sent word by his disciples to Jesus, asking, ³ "Are you the one who is to come, or should we look for another?"

4 Jesus responded, "Go, report to John what you hear and see.

5 Those who were blind are able to see. Those who were crippled are walking. People with skin diseases are cleansed. Those who were deaf now hear. Those who were dead are raised up. The poor have good news proclaimed to them.

6 Happy are those who don't stumble and fall because of me."

7 When John's disciples had gone, Jesus spoke to the crowds about John: "What did you go out to the wilderness to see? A stalk blowing in the wind?

8 What did you go out to see? A man dressed up in refined clothes? Look, those who wear refined clothes are in royal palaces.

9 What did you go out to see? A prophet? Yes, I tell you, and more than a prophet.

10 He is the one of whom it is written: Look, I'm sending my messenger before you, who will prepare your way before you.

11 "I assure you that no one who has ever been born is greater than John the Baptist. Yet whoever is least in the kingdom of heaven is greater than he.

12 From the days of John the Baptist until now the kingdom of heaven is violently attacked as violent people seize it.

13 All the Prophets and the Law prophesied until John came.

14 If you are willing to accept it, he is Elijah who is to come.

15 Let the person who has ears, hear.

Matthew 12:1-14

1 At that time Jesus went through the wheat fields on the Sabbath. His disciples were hungry so they were picking heads of wheat and eating them.

2 When the Pharisees saw this, they said to him, "Look, your disciples are breaking the Sabbath law."

3 But he said to them, "Haven't you read what David did when he and those with him were hungry?

4 He went into God's house and broke the law by eating the bread of the presence, which only the priests were allowed to eat.

5 Or haven't you read in the Law that on the Sabbath the priests in the temple treat the Sabbath as any other day and are still innocent?

6 But I tell you that something greater than the temple is here.

7 If you had known what this means, I want mercy and not sacrifice, you wouldn't have condemned the innocent.

8 The Human One is Lord of the Sabbath."

9 Jesus left that place and went into their synagogue.

10 A man with a withered hand was there. Wanting to bring charges against Jesus, they asked, "Does the Law allow a person to heal on the Sabbath?"

11 Jesus replied, "Who among you has a sheep that falls into a pit on the Sabbath and will not take hold of it and pull it out?

12 How much more valuable is a person than a sheep! So the Law allows a person to do what is good on the Sabbath."

13 Then Jesus said to the man, "Stretch out your hand." So he did and it was made healthy, just like the other one.

14 The Pharisees went out and met in order to find a way to destroy Jesus.

Key words or phrases?

Insights?

Matthew 12:22-32

22 They brought to Jesus a demon-possessed man who was blind and unable to speak. Jesus healed him so that he could both speak and see.

23 All the crowds were amazed and said, "This man couldn't be the Son of David, could he?"

24 When the Pharisees heard, they said, "This man throws out demons only by the authority of Beelzebul, the ruler of the demons."

25 Because Jesus knew what they were thinking, he replied, "Every kingdom involved in civil war becomes a wasteland. Every city or house torn apart by divisions will collapse.

26 If Satan throws out Satan, he is at war with himself. How then can his kingdom endure?

27 And if I throw out demons by the authority of Beelzebul, then by whose authority do your followers throw them out? Therefore, they will be your judges.

28 But if I throw out demons by the power of God's Spirit, then God's kingdom has already overtaken you.

29 Can people go into a house that belongs to a strong man and steal his possessions, unless they first tie up the strong man? Then they can rob his house.

30 Whoever isn't with me is against me, and whoever doesn't gather with me scatters.

31   "Therefore, I tell you that people will be forgiven for every sin and insult to God. But insulting the Holy Spirit won't be forgiven.

32   And whoever speaks a word against the Human One will be forgiven. But whoever speaks against the Holy Spirit won't be forgiven, not in this age or in the age that is coming.

Key words or phrases?

Insights?

Matthew 13:1-9, 18-23

1 That day Jesus went out of the house and sat down beside the lake.

2 Such large crowds gathered around him that he climbed into a boat and sat down. The whole crowd was standing on the shore.

3 He said many things to them in parables: "A farmer went out to scatter seed.

4 As he was scattering seed, some fell on the path, and birds came and ate it.

5 Other seed fell on rocky ground where the soil was shallow. They sprouted immediately because the soil wasn't deep.

6 But when the sun came up, it scorched the plants, and they dried up because they had no roots.

7 Other seed fell among thorny plants. The thorny plants grew and choked them.

8 Other seed fell on good soil and bore fruit, in one case a yield of one hundred to one, in another case a yield of sixty to one, and in another case a yield of thirty to one.

9 Everyone who has ears should pay attention."

18 "Consider then the parable of the farmer.

19   Whenever people hear the word about the kingdom and don't understand it, the evil one comes and carries off what was planted in their hearts. This is the seed that was sown on the path.

20   As for the seed that was spread on rocky ground, this refers to people who hear the word and immediately receive it joyfully.

21   Because they have no roots, they last for only a little while. When they experience distress or abuse because of the word, they immediately fall away.

22   As for the seed that was spread among thorny plants, this refers to those who hear the word, but the worries of this life and the false appeal of wealth choke the word, and it bears no fruit.

23   As for what was planted on good soil, this refers to those who hear and understand, and bear fruit and produce—in one case a yield of one hundred to one, in another case a yield of sixty to one, and in another case a yield of thirty to one."

Key words or phrases?

Insights?

Matthew 13:10-17, 31-35

10 Jesus' disciples came and said to him, "Why do you use parables when you speak to the crowds?"

11 Jesus replied, "Because they haven't received the secrets of the kingdom of heaven, but you have.

12 For those who have will receive more and they will have more than enough. But as for those who don't have, even the little they have will be taken away from them.

13 This is why I speak to the crowds in parables: although they see, they don't really see; and although they hear, they don't really hear or understand.

14 What Isaiah prophesied has become completely true for them:

You will hear, to be sure, but never understand;
and you will certainly see but never recognize what you
are seeing.

15 For this people's senses have become calloused,
and they've become hard of hearing,
and they've shut their eyes
so that they won't see with their eyes
or hear with their ears
or understand with their minds,
and change their hearts and lives that I may heal them.

16 "Happy are your eyes because they see. Happy are your ears because they hear.

17 I assure you that many prophets and righteous people wanted to see what you see and hear what you hear, but they didn't.

31 He told another parable to them: "The kingdom of heaven is like a mustard seed that someone took and planted in his field.

32 It's the smallest of all seeds. But when it's grown, it's the largest of all vegetable plants. It becomes a tree so that the birds in the sky come and nest in its branches."

33 He told them another parable: "The kingdom of heaven is like yeast, which a woman took and hid in a bushel of wheat flour until the yeast had worked its way through all the dough."

34 Jesus said all these things to the crowds in parables, and he spoke to them only in parables.

35 This was to fulfill what the prophet spoke:

I'll speak in parables;
I'll declare what has been hidden since the beginning of the world.

Key words or phrases?

Insights?

Matthew 13:24-30, 36-43

24   Jesus told them another parable: "The kingdom of heaven is like someone who planted good seed in his field.

25   While people were sleeping, an enemy came and planted weeds among the wheat and went away.

26   When the stalks sprouted and bore grain, then the weeds also appeared.

27   "The servants of the landowner came and said to him, 'Master, didn't you plant good seed in your field? Then how is it that it has weeds?'

28   "'An enemy has done this,' he answered. "The servants said to him, 'Do you want us to go and gather them?'

29   "But the landowner said, 'No, because if you gather the weeds, you'll pull up the wheat along with them.

30   Let both grow side by side until the harvest. And at harvesttime I'll say to the harvesters, "First gather the weeds and tie them together in bundles to be burned. But bring the wheat into my barn." '"

36   Jesus left the crowds and went into the house. His disciples came to him and said, "Explain to us the parable of the weeds in the field."

37   Jesus replied, "The one who plants the good seed is the Human One.

38 The field is the world. And the good seeds are the followers of the kingdom. But the weeds are the followers of the evil one.

39 The enemy who planted them is the devil. The harvest is the end of the present age. The harvesters are the angels.

40 Just as people gather weeds and burn them in the fire, so it will be at the end of the present age.

41 The Human One will send his angels, and they will gather out of his kingdom all things that cause people to fall away and all people who sin.

42 He will throw them into a burning furnace. People there will be weeping and grinding their teeth.

43 Then the righteous will shine like the sun in their Father's kingdom. Those who have ears should hear."

Matthew 13:44-53

[44] "The kingdom of heaven is like a treasure that somebody hid in a field, which someone else found and covered up. Full of joy, the finder sold everything and bought that field.

[45] "Again, the kingdom of heaven is like a merchant in search of fine pearls.

[46] When he found one very precious pearl, he went and sold all that he owned and bought it.

[47] "Again, the kingdom of heaven is like a net that people threw into the lake and gathered all kinds of fish.

[48] When it was full, they pulled it to the shore, where they sat down and put the good fish together into containers. But the bad fish they threw away.

[49] That's the way it will be at the end of the present age. The angels will go out and separate the evil people from the righteous people, [50] and will throw the evil ones into a burning furnace. People there will be weeping and grinding their teeth.

[51] "Have you understood all these things?" Jesus asked. They said to him, "Yes."

[52] Then he said to them, "Therefore, every legal expert who has been trained as a disciple for the kingdom of heaven is like the head of a household who brings old and new things out of their treasure chest."

[53] When Jesus finished these parables, he departed.

Key words or phrases?

Insights?

Matthew 13:54–14:12

⁵⁴ When he came to his hometown, he taught the people in their synagogue. They were surprised and said, "Where did he get this wisdom? Where did he get the power to work miracles?

⁵⁵ Isn't he the carpenter's son? Isn't his mother named Mary? Aren't James, Joseph, Simon, and Judas his brothers?

⁵⁶ And his sisters, aren't they here with us? Where did this man get all this?"

⁵⁷ They were repulsed by him and fell into sin.

But Jesus said to them, "Prophets are honored everywhere except in their own hometowns and in their own households." 58 He was unable to do many miracles there because of their disbelief.

¹ At that time Herod the ruler heard the news about Jesus.

² He said to his servants, "This is John the Baptist. He's been raised from the dead. This is why these miraculous powers are at work through him."

³ Herod had arrested John, bound him, and put him in prison because of Herodias, the wife of Herod's brother Philip.

⁴ That's because John told Herod, "It's against the law for you to marry her."

⁵ Although Herod wanted to kill him, he feared the crowd because they thought John was a prophet.

6   But at Herod's birthday party Herodias' daughter danced in front of the guests and thrilled Herod.

7   Then he swore to give her anything she asked.

8   At her mother's urging, the girl said, "Give me the head of John the Baptist here on a plate."

9   Although the king was upset, because of his solemn pledge and his guests he commanded that they give it to her.

10 Then he had John beheaded in prison.

11 They brought his head on a plate and gave it to the young woman, and she brought it to her mother.

12 But John's disciples came and took his body and buried it. Then they went and told Jesus what had happened.

Key words or phrases?

Insights?

Matthew 14:13-21

13 When Jesus heard about John, he withdrew in a boat to a deserted place by himself. When the crowds learned this, they followed him on foot from the cities.

14 When Jesus arrived and saw a large crowd, he had compassion for them and healed those who were sick.

15 That evening his disciples came and said to him, "This is an isolated place and it's getting late. Send the crowds away so they can go into the villages and buy food for themselves."

16 But Jesus said to them, "There's no need to send them away. You give them something to eat."

17 They replied, "We have nothing here except five loaves of bread and two fish."

18 He said, "Bring them here to me."

19 He ordered the crowds to sit down on the grass. He took the five loaves of bread and the two fish, looked up to heaven, blessed them and broke the loaves apart and gave them to his disciples. Then the disciples gave them to the crowds.

20 Everyone ate until they were full, and they filled twelve baskets with the leftovers.

21 About five thousand men plus women and children had eaten.

Key words or phrases?

Insights?

Matthew 14:22-33

22 Right then, Jesus made the disciples get into the boat and go ahead to the other side of the lake while he dismissed the crowds.

23 When he sent them away, he went up onto a mountain by himself to pray. Evening came and he was alone.

24 Meanwhile, the boat, fighting a strong headwind, was being battered by the waves and was already far away from land.

25 Very early in the morning he came to his disciples, walking on the lake.

26 When the disciples saw him walking on the lake, they were terrified and said, "It's a ghost!" They were so frightened they screamed.

27 Just then Jesus spoke to them, "Be encouraged! It's me. Don't be afraid."

28 Peter replied, "Lord, if it's you, order me to come to you on the water."

29 And Jesus said, "Come." Then Peter got out of the boat and was walking on the water toward Jesus.

30 But when Peter saw the strong wind, he became frightened. As he began to sink, he shouted, "Lord, rescue me!"

31 Jesus immediately reached out and grabbed him, saying, "You man of weak faith! Why did you begin to have doubts?"

32   When they got into the boat, the wind settled down.

33   Then those in the boat worshipped Jesus and said, "You must be God's Son!"

Key words or phrases?

Insights?

Matthew 15:1-20

1 Then Pharisees and legal experts came to Jesus from Jerusalem and said, 2 "Why are your disciples breaking the elders' rules handed down to us? They don't ritually purify their hands by washing before they eat."

3 Jesus replied, "Why do you break the command of God by keeping the rules handed down to you?

4 For God said, Honor your father and your mother, and The person who speaks against father or mother will certainly be put to death.

5 But you say, 'If you tell your father or mother, "Everything I'm expected to contribute to you I'm giving to God as a gift," then you don't have to honor your father.'

6 So you do away with God's Law for the sake of the rules that have been handed down to you.

7 Hypocrites! Isaiah really knew what he was talking about when he prophesied about you,

8 This people honors me with their lips, but their hearts are far away from me.

9 Their worship of me is empty since they teach instructions that are human rules."

10 Jesus called the crowd near and said to them, "Listen and understand.

11   It's not what goes into the mouth that contaminates a person in God's sight. It's what comes out of the mouth that contaminates the person."

12   Then the disciples came and said to him, "Do you know that the Pharisees were offended by what you just said?"

13   Jesus replied, "Every plant that my heavenly Father didn't plant will be pulled up.

14   Leave the Pharisees alone. They are blind people who are guides to blind people. But if a blind person leads another blind person, they will both fall into a ditch."

15   Then Peter spoke up, "Explain this riddle to us."

16   Jesus said, "Don't you understand yet?

17   Don't you know that everything that goes into the mouth enters the stomach and goes out into the sewer?

18   But what goes out of the mouth comes from the heart. And that's what contaminates a person in God's sight.

19   Out of the heart come evil thoughts, murders, adultery, sexual sins, thefts, false testimonies, and insults.

20   These contaminate a person in God's sight. But eating without washing hands doesn't contaminate in God's sight."

Key words or phrases?

Insights?

Made in the USA
Columbia, SC
09 July 2019